GOING
THE
EXTRA MILE

Engaging your workforce to grow profit!

With thanks to writers Chris Humphreys and Alison Clements

Sub-editors – Dawn Leahey and Michelle Johnson

Designed by Brilliant Ltd

Published by The Extra Mile Partnership Ltd

The Extra Mile Partnership Ltd.
F17 Allen House
The Maltings
Station Road
Sawbridgeworth
Hertfordshire
CM21 9JX

First published by The Extra Mile Partnership Ltd. 2009

British Library Cataloguing in Publication Data. A cataloguing record for this book is available from the British Library.

ISBN 978-0-9553356-6-2

Typeset in Gill Sans by www.brilliant.ltd.uk

Printed and bound in Great Britain by Bell Press – www.bell-press.co.uk

Dedications

To my late grandfather Jack, for showing me how to have gratitude, the right attitude and to always pursue the extra mile.

For the two kings of customer service, Julian Richer and Charles Dunstone, who have had so much influence on how I care for colleagues and customers and who inspired me to follow the path towards good profits.

Thanks to the truly exceptional Extra Mile team, Chris, Dawn, Steve and Michelle, whose genuine care for our clients and their businesses I'm eternally grateful for, and without whom this book would not be possible.

Contents

"The purpose of this book is to tackle the issues that every business leader needs to grasp if they wish to spearhead a high performance culture geared to sustainable growth."

Introduction

A successful business creates opportunities for leaders and colleagues alike to shine and grow, to smile, to enthuse, to feel good about themselves and radiate their feelings to customers, friends and family. Success is contagious, it drives a healthy economy and just makes life sweet.

A failing business harms all it touches, drains energy, breeds insecurity and fear, compromises work and family relationships, threatens livelihoods, challenges good behaviour, undermines public spiritedness and just makes life sour.

In an economic downturn, astute leaders plan for life beyond the trading lull. Successful businesses will emerge from the recession having mustered strength and galvanised colleagues ready for sustained growth in the future. This kind of corporate vision surely needs to have employee engagement running through it. Engaged, motivated staff will perform better, the customers will benefit from great customer service, and more money will come through the tills. Enlightened CEOs and HR directors know this mantra well.

But what exactly does employee engagement look like? Should you start top-down or go straight to the shop floor? What ROI can you expect? Most importantly, how can you measure every step of the journey so that improvements can be celebrated and built upon? In this harsh economic climate, having the answers to these questions has never been so important.

If you're in it for the long term, then so am I.

The Light that Shines Twice as Bright Shines Half as Long

More and more businesses that I get called into are operating in a climate where the predominant KPI that measures success is like-for-like sales. I am often asked to put together short term strategies and punchy training programmes that focus upon delivering this measure. 'Flavour of the month' training can be highly effective and, because it is so aligned to short term results, easily judged from a ROI perspective. Delivering this is like falling off a log for me.

But while I have a huge appetite to add value to all my clients' balance sheets, I struggle with the concept of artificial flavourings. There is one simple question that I always ask every client before I even consider working on a short term fix – is the business chasing good profits or bad profits?

Good Profits or Bad Profits?

In his book The Ultimate Question, US business strategist and loyalty expert Frederick Reichheld coined the terms 'bad' and 'good' profits. The former are earned at the expense of the customer, the latter are earned with the customer's enthusiastic cooperation. Bad profits are corporate steroids that boost short-term earnings but burn out employees and alienate customers.

If however, a business builds a sequence of engaged relationships of such high quality that those relationships breed an army of loyal customers who are 'promoters', these will generate good profits and fuel sustainable growth. Thank you and high five to you Fred.

In my opinion, sustainable growth is the trophy to play for in the competition for success. The winners are those organizations that trade on honest relationships in which colleagues feel safe, trusted and cared for. In common with the colleagues, the customers share a desire for the brand to do well thus contributing to an uptake in market share and shareholder value.

Over the last 14 years, I have made it my business to contribute to a number of trophy-winning organizations. My team and I have been able to tap into the DNA of these winning organizations, capture the sequence, model it and reproduce it for the benefit of all my clients. We've discovered it's more time and cost effective to build a company culture around relationships and behaviours that last, rather than relying on 'flavour of the month' interventions that ultimately yield bad profits. I call this the 'Extra Mile Model'.

Measuring the Extra Mile

The outcome of our Extra Mile Model is the ability to satisfy softer HR objectives around engagement and job satisfaction, while surpassing the robust ROI targets set by the CEO. What makes our way of working different from others in the market is our focus on measuring all these elements.

Building a high performance culture based on engagement involves an initial investment in 'intangibles'; attitude, behaviour, vision, courage, determination and fun. I am here to tell you that in constructing such a culture you must and can adopt perpetual systems of measurement that will give you indications of success and ROI every step of the way.

In this book – a one hour read – I will detail how we can help you accurately measure colleague attitudes, the outcome of training, and customer experience. Where these 'softer' measures begin growing exponentially, improvements in harder measures follow.

One client – an international retail company – saw the following results in a problematic store over a 20-week period, once colleagues had been through an Extra Mile training programme, embracing a culture of engagement and best practise:

From not reaching target in the previous 30 weeks, it hit target for 21 out of the next 22 weeks. Sales increased versus budget by over £500k in 20 weeks. The store achieved over £1 million showroom sales per month against an average target of £734k per month.

The extra mile culture within the store became incredibly strong and was passed on to new recruits because existing colleagues passionately believed in the new 'Customer is King' ethos. Staff enjoyed new levels of job satisfaction and feelings of empowerment, attendance levels rose, shrinkage decreased and staff turnover improved. All these KPIs were measured and assigned a per head value.

The MD calculated that in one year alone, by increasing employee engagement from 1 in 3, to 1 in 7 disengaged colleagues, his company liberated an extra £100 million of resources.

Industry figures tell a similar tale. Research by the Corporate Leadership Council equates a 10% rise in engagement to a 6% increase in effort, which in turn leads to at least an extra 2% increase in performance.

Where Are You?

Employee engagement is not an exact science but I do know that there is proof, in every organisation in which I have worked, that increased engagement equates to a significantly improved business performance; better sales, recurring revenues, world class customer relationship management, less attrition, less absenteeism, lower shrinkage and less resource spent on employee disciplinaries and disputes.

Only you will know the potential value that highly engaged colleagues could add to each of your key performance measures. But I would suggest it's an incredibly worthwhile, eye-opening calculation to perform.

The purpose of this book is to tackle the issues that every business leader needs to grasp if they wish to spearhead a high performance culture geared to sustainable growth. I hope the outcome of this book is for you to decide whether the pursuit of good profits – going the extra mile – is for you.

"Is it just me that believes that the 'old fashioned' virtues of humility, trust, responsibility, gratitude, honesty and loyalty are needed more now than ever before?"

Chapter 1
Why The Extra Mile?

Grandad Jack

I've always been fascinated by the way colleague culture can impact upon the profits and sustainability of a business. My interest harks back to my late grandfather, Jack Becker, who ran several pubs around South East London, including the famous Windmill in Soho. He loved life, and it showed in the way he ran his business. He was in the pub from 6.30am to midnight, making sure the cellar was in order, and treating his customers with such good intent that it felt like a second home to them. He influenced them in a very positive way, and as a result his customers were incredibly loyal, coming back time and again.

I remember asking my grandfather what he would do if someone was to get drunk and aggressive. He simply gestured in the direction of his bar staff and customers and said, 'it's our pub this is. They'll help me sort it, son!'

What a thought – your customers managing your business with you! Grandad Jack was an 'extra miler', and his staff and customers couldn't be more engaged. Is it just me that believes that the 'old fashioned' virtues of humility, trust, responsibility, gratitude, honesty and loyalty are needed more now than ever before? I don't think so.

Hard Lessons

Personal experiences of the highs and lows of running a business shape my thinking today. At the age of 29 I'd reached my goal of making a million, but my publishing business was facing bankruptcy and my health had nose-dived. I'd excelled at chasing bad profits at the expense of good profits.

I had an aggressive team of commission-only salespeople whose job was to sell advertising space. Instead of genuinely seeking to meet the needs of our advertisers, I encouraged my people to promise whatever it took to sell the space. My vision was coloured by short-term gain, which I felt would best deliver the numbers demanded of me by the investors in my business. This strategy meant that my clients didn't get the level of response that they were expecting from advertising with us and therefore didn't re-book.

I worked relentlessly to bring my company back from bankruptcy, putting in 12–16 hour days and straining my personal relationships in the process. I eventually succeeded, but at serious risk to my health. I had discovered a growth on my neck and, though I tried to ignore it, I was eventually persuaded by my sister to go to my GP.

I was diagnosed with Hodgkin's Disease, a form of cancer that attacks the body's lymphatic system. My doctor gave me a dire prognosis, estimating that I had just 12 weeks to live, and I was soon fired by my investors due to my illness.

For Richer and Poorer

At my lowest point, my friend Julian Richer, Founder of Richer Sounds, Britain's biggest hi-fi retailer, took it upon himself to arrange for me to meet some new doctors. Their integrated treatments ultimately helped me make a full recovery, against the odds.

I had first met Julian at an event where he was presenting a keynote speech, and having had some speaking experience, I introduced myself with a view to sharing some ideas. We clicked instantly and our friendship flourished. When I found my company was in need of entrepreneurial skill, it was Julian who made a bid to buy out the bank that had invested in it. When I finally recovered from my illness, it was Julian who offered me a job with his telesales department, getting me back in the game.

Working with Julian made me understand that there were highly successful people in big business who also genuinely cared for others. Like my grandfather Jack, he valued his people, his customers and his profits. He was a fully paid-up member of the extra mile club.

66 *People don't care how much you know until they know how much you care.* **99**
Dale Carnegie

The Richer Way

Being immersed in the 'Richer Way' was a baptism for me. I had never worked in an organization where colleagues and customers shared such a mutual love for the brand, nor had I experienced such a workplace buzz. But being a sceptical bugger, I wondered whether these intangible 'feel goods' were merely anecdotal or actually impacted in real terms upon performance.

To this day, the facts continue to speak for themselves. Richer Sounds has for 15 years, according to the Guinness Book of Records, enjoyed the highest sales per square foot of any retailer in the world. It also boasts an annual shrinkage rate of 0.2% which compares to the average shrinkage rate in the retail sector of 1.6%. And if I were to tell you that the British Retail Consortium (Retail Crime Costs Survey) equates a 1.6% shrinkage rate to a loss in profit of circa 17.8%, then we can start to attach a meaningful value to employee engagement.

Turbo-charging the Extra Mile

66 *A leader has the vision and conviction that a dream can be achieved. He inspires the power and energy to get it done.* **99**

Ralph Nader

Every customer-facing organization has hotspots where excellent relationships are positively impacting upon results. How many times have you thought 'if only all my outlets/teams could be like that one?' and wondered how to duplicate it?

From what I've seen, sustainability and consistency throughout an organisation can only be driven top down. Julian Richer has personally set out the extra mile route for colleagues to follow. His behaviour turbo-charges from the top of Richer Sounds and generates enough power throughout the hierarchy to the front line where a customer's first experience of his brand is ignited.

Why the Extra Mile? I believe it's what we should all aspire to.

Building 'good profits' leads to 'on-brand' employees and customers who actively want the business to succeed.

Pursuing only 'bad profits' causes inconsistent behaviours, dissatisfaction and diminishing returns.

Has anyone inspired you in the way they run their business? If so, how?

Can you envisage the power of an Extra Mile culture within your organisation?

"Your company will not reach anywhere near its full potential if all that is guiding it is a list of pleasant platitudes hanging on the lobby wall..."

Bring Mission Statements To Life

In his book 'Winning', Jack Welch, ex-Chairman and CEO of General Electric, says:

> *Your company will not reach anywhere near its full potential if all that is guiding it is a list of pleasant platitudes hanging on the lobby wall... Your mission statement and values need time spent on them, and they need to be made real.*

I'm sure we all agree with big Jack. Yet when my company conducted a survey of Britain's top 200 retailers in January 2009, less than 9% of the frontline colleagues we asked, had any idea of what their company's mission statement was.

One financial services company I worked with had spent £30k sending its senior management team to a Bavarian castle to 'brainstorm' a new mission statement! But bringing it alive from the ivory tower to the shop floor proved to be the real challenge.

Quite simply, your mission statement must be lived by every colleague, from CEO to grassroots level, and experienced by every customer. Your statement should be as meaningful in the lobby as it is in the boardroom, as it is in the works canteen, giving rise to behaviours that can be lived and policed at all levels.

> *Weak leadership creates a disgruntled and resentful workforce and, sooner or later, service to the customer will suffer.*
>
> **Julian Richer**

Attitude Not Platitude

By way of testing the validity of Welch's argument let's look at the Richer Sounds mission:

> *To provide second-to-none service and value for money for our customers.*
>
> *To provide ourselves with secure, well-paid jobs working in a stimulating and equal opportunities environment.*
>
> *To be profitable to ensure long term growth and survival.*

Great. But the clever part is enabling this crystal clear Extra Mile roadmap to actually guide the behaviours and performance of the organization.

Well, here's how Richer Sounds makes it happen. Right from induction, colleagues learn that outstanding service and value for money for the customer drives the entire business. The company pays well for hard-working brand ambassadors who deliver results. Company benefits are fun and attractive, such as the use of company holiday homes and free massages. The working environment is constantly evolving so is stimulating, Corporate Social Responsibility is taken seriously with a percentage of profits dedicated to its charitable foundation, there are profit share opportunities for colleagues. The suggestion scheme really works: Julian reads each one, and those that would provide a positive benefit for future improvement are implemented. Colleagues are empowered and respected.

Crucially, success is measured. Colleague motivation and job satisfaction are measured regularly through a colleague attitude survey. The level of excellence of customer service is targeted above 90% for the company as a whole. Again, this is measured through real-time customer feedback channels such as till receipt questionnaires.

Need I go on? The spine of Richer Sounds' operating system is engagement. It is an intrinsically motivated workforce where shrinkage is 0.2% – roughly 10% of the industry average! And its culture is turbo-charged in both word and deed, from the top.

Carphone Warehouse

I have also experienced a similar character ethic at Carphone Warehouse, where founder and Chairman Charles Dunstone treats his colleagues as he would wish to be treated – one of 'Five Fundamental Rules' that govern relationships and behaviour throughout CPW.

My team and I have carried out training at different levels in this company and have learnt a great deal about a culture where a duty of care for colleagues is passed on to customers. CPW is also ground-breaking in its approach to capturing and using data on the customer experience, and aligning colleague behaviour accordingly.

The CPW customer metric – which is being made available to colleagues daily in all shops – forms part of a balanced scorecard that is used to remunerate the colleagues accordingly. Customer centric behaviour, which is one of the cornerstones of good profits, is rewarded alongside the volume of sales made.

Now I'm not saying that Charles or Julian have perfect systems, but both place the potential for long term value creation, or good profits, above the short term vagaries of stock market fashions. Both know what it takes to set the pace.

Mission statements should promote a character ethic and give rise to behaviours that can be lived and policed at all levels.

Are you entirely happy with your existing Mission Statement today?

Are its values actively played out by colleagues across the organisation?

How familiar with their Mission Statement are your staff?

How often are suggestions from employees implemented and celebrated?

Chapter 3
Digging for Victory

Whenever I begin a new project with a company, my team and I undertake a process called 'digging', where we seek to reveal the root causes of an organisation's challenges and custom build a platform for effective solutions. Treating the causes allows a company to instigate a new high performance culture equipped for sustainability; treating the symptoms offers the path of least resistance for all involved but will usually result in a short term fix.

> **66** *However beautiful the strategy, you should occasionally look at the results.* **99**
> **Sir Winston Churchill**

A thorough 'dig' involves speaking to people at every level of an organisation, to temperature check the quality of relationships and behaviours and the systems through which they are communicated. Are frontline staff given the opportunity to channel their ideas to the board? Is current behaviour is in line with the vision? Do colleagues at all levels feel the company cares about them?

So what does effective digging look like and what are the most common challenges that this process unearths?

> **66** *The only man who behaved sensibly was my tailor; he took my measurement anew every time he saw me, while all the rest went on with their old measurements and expected them to fit me.* **99**
> **George Bernard Shaw**

Digging Up the 7 Deadliest Sins

Through many years of spadework, I have excavated the most common issues that plague customer-facing enterprises and are the primary causes of inability to generate good profit. These are:

Poor leadership

Ineffective communication

Lack of clarity & accountability around targets & measurements

High levels of disengagement

Disproportionate hours spent on task rather than service

Reactive salesmanship/customer service

Poor quality of sale

The correlations are obvious and spiral downwards: Poor leaders communicate ineffectively; they often set sales and performance targets that do not take into account measurements of colleague and customer attitudes and behaviours; ignored or misunderstood colleagues makes them de-motivated which in turn leads to uncertainty, lack of confidence and ultimately disengagement; disengaged colleagues will then lose the desire to proactively charm and build relationships with customers, which adversely affects the quality of sales.

I heartily recommend applying a number of interventions that are guaranteed to reveal the true state of play in any organisation.

Attitude Surveys

❝*Attitude is a little thing that makes a big difference.*❞
Sir Winston Churchill

If someone is feeling unhappy or undervalued, how do you know? The bottom line is that unless you have two-way communication on a regular basis with your colleagues, the judgment calls that you make may be inappropriate for their needs.

In any team-building environment, honest and respectful feedback is a must. I have coached CEOs and football managers alike, who have been adamant that they were portraying a set of behaviours that their teams should emulate. In such scenarios, my job was to uncover and remedy the push and pull between leader and teams which had been resulting in a lack of unity and poor results.

The attitude survey is a powerful digging tool because it can be so accurately calibrated – by department, by job title, by locality, by question type and so on. Not only can it be used to flush out concerns, it can also be used to capture the attitudes and behaviours where best practice is prevalent.

When I work with a company, I like to demonstrate the value of regular attitude surveys to the business, the results of which can be cost effectively monitored and measured.

Encourage through One-to-Ones

A 'normal' one-to-one, in an appraisal or performance review situation, involves pointing out some good attributes of your colleague, then suggesting where they need to improve and finishing on a few more good things to ensure they don't leave in a bad mood. Box ticked.

I view this as wasting a valuable opportunity. To my mind, the one-to-one is about drawing from the colleague how they feel and what their aspirations are. Normally, 9 out of 10 people want to do a good job and will be harder on themselves than their line manager could ever be, as long as they are treated with care, respect and dignity.

The power of the one-to-one comes from the colleague describing their attributes and how they are going to use them. By encouraging your colleagues to behave proactively, they will learn how to become part of the solution for the business, meeting the needs of the business while learning how to work better, smarter and harder. If you do no more than listen with sincere interest to people, your relationships and effectiveness with them will grow immensely.

Real Time Customer Feedback

I asked the manager of a large retailer we were working with: 'What do your customers think of you?' In response he handed me the Mystery Shopping results of his store. Historically, mystery shopping had been the primary source for service feedback (as it is to many customer-facing companies).

I'm convinced there can be drawbacks inherent in this methodology.

Choice of supplier and how they recruit and incentivise their shoppers is key here. Colleagues can often identify who mystery shoppers are by their techniques, the questions they ask, and soon inform one another, thus skewing any potential results.

Also, you need to be aware that a low volume of mystery shops conducted per outlet or colleague can only give a snapshot of the overall offering. I have worked with a corporation that would perform 100,000 transactions per month; they would experience one mystery shop per month, providing feedback about a single colleague performing a single transaction. Utterly unrepresentative.

The aim of a customer feedback measure should be to question the biggest number and widest selection of customers possible about the service they receive – whether they have bought from you or not - then to feed the results back quickly down the line where the learnings can be acted upon.

One of the methods we recommend is Fred Reichheld's Net Promoter Score (NPS) – a much faster, accurate way of gauging customers' real loyalty to a company which introduces a quantitative measure (the NPS) for establishing a baseline and effectively tracking changes going forward. At the heart of the metric is what is known as the 'ultimate question'. Customers are asked the following question and answer it on a scale from 1 to 10: Would you recommend us to your friends and family?

By measuring the level of customer/client satisfaction, businesses are able to assess their own effectiveness in the marketplace. Net Promoter Score offers a rapid call to action and, if embedded as a discipline in organisations, can be used to foster growth and 'good' profitability.

When my team asked the 'ultimate question' as part of a client experience survey with a merchant bank, the surprising rush of negative results made it immediately apparent that the level of client delight was severely lacking. The by-product of this had been ineffective client retention and disunity amongst team members when pitching for new business. However, the candid feedback forced the management team and colleagues to face the truth and, with support and training, take control of it.

Measure Colleague to Colleague Experience

Many of my clients are using similar methodology described above on themselves. In one such example, each of the team members is asked to rank order all the others, from best to worst, based on the quality of the customer service they have given over the previous week. Each team member is asked to explain the thinking behind their rankings in a constructive manner, providing specific examples of best and worst practise (e.g. 'David's uniform was regularly grubby this week', 'Lisa's ability to make eye contact and smile with customers has been legendary' etc.). The collated scores are visible to all the team and the highest scorer each week is rewarded.

This system for self-policing behaviours has worked wonders. The benchmark for high quality relationships has been set high, engagement levels have progressively improved and, not surprisingly, ATV is peaking. The value to this retailer of decreasing attrition, absenteeism and shrinkage levels is phenomenal.

Pack in Pigeon Visits

Be wary of the 'Pigeon Visit'. A delegation of, say, the Regional Manager, Sales Director and Retail Manager march into a store, or depot, pick holes, ruffle a few feathers, and leave everyone with the sense they've been shat on. They don't acknowledge colleagues but will highlight everything that is not in line with expected procedures, from the wonky promo poster to the gaps on the shelves, to dusty marks on the floor.

In my experience, when top-to middle-management visit their branches/ outlets, they often behave in a way that is the total antithesis of what is expected at the business/customer interface. They don't engage, communicate and encourage.

When undertaking those visits, if those at the top of the chain cannot be bothered to lead by example and align themselves with their company's mission statement, where's the intrinsic motivation for client-facing colleagues to do so? I call this the 'Willie Walsh factor':

Following the troubled opening of Heathrow's Terminal 5 in May 2008, the CEO of British Airways, Willie Walsh declined his annual bonus despite the airline posting record profits. Willie said he felt any award would have been "inappropriate" given the problem-hit move to the new building.

I would highly commend Willie for simply doing what's right and setting a virtuous precedent for today's evolutionary trading conditions.

Talk to People at the Coalface

❝I believe you learn most about an organisation from talking to its staff.❞
Julian Richer

At the digging stage, store visits are a valuable information gathering exercise. They should always be people-centric and should be conducted through the eyes of the colleague and the customer. Take time to serve customers and ask for their feedback – this way, you will be able to understand the customer experience from a personal perspective rather than make assumptions based on information from a balance sheet. Get talking in order to understand the needs of your people and focus on the people performance of the outlet/department/team you are visiting.

A thorough dig, using some or all of the interventions above, will position you to decide whether you and your colleagues are fit and willing to go the extra mile and enter the competition for good profits.

A process of 'digging' helps us unearth the quality of relationships and communication systems across a client business.

When was the last time you temperature-checked staff attitudes across the business, acted upon the results and measured on-going progress?

Could your appraisals be used more effectively?

Do frontline staff in your organisation feel management understand their needs and concerns?

How would your company fare if you introduced the Net Promoter Score or similar metric?

Chapter 4
Uniting The Forces

In my company's Extra Mile Model, 'digging' is followed by what we call 'uniting the forces'. This is where we begin to action change in a business.

Management statements such as 'our people are our biggest asset' simply aren't powerful enough to unite forces across a large company. Action is needed, and this means the installation of behaviours, systems and processes that bring a company's mission statement and values to life. This is why we partner with our clients to bespoke a real time performance management system that keeps the actions alive, monitors progress and measures return on investment.

❝ *The way to get started is to quit talking and begin doing.* **❞**
Walt Disney

Mis-Leading by Example

I love it when the senior management teams I work with join in my training sessions with verve and energy – such a public show of commitment is a great starting point for building reciprocal high quality relationships.

Adversely, I have known plenty of stakeholders and sponsors that want to sit at the back of the training room in an 'observational' (aka 'cop out') capacity. What sort of message does this send out to the team? That their bosses were too good for the training?

Uniting the forces is about stakeholder vision and visibility which needs to be consistently percolated from the very top, to the front line. A strong network of extra mile ambassadors are essential for the job.

Extra Mile Ambassadors

❝ *The vision is really about empowering workers, giving them all the information about what's going on so they can do a lot more than they've done in the past.* **❞**
                                                                   Bill Gates

Jack Welch believes that real 'change agents' comprise less than 10% of all business people. It's these 10% that will convince the 70-80% of 'neutrals' that change is worth it. So during the 'uniting the forces' process it's essential to identify and empower your real agents for change. These purveyors of best practice need to be mobilised and cloned. Capture their ideas and send them out to educate others.

When advising clients, I always seek to identify such individuals and put them through an intensive programme where they become accredited in my Extra Mile methodology. They are then returned to the business as the definitive ambassadors for sustainable change and peak performance.

The methodology that they learn is far from a trade secret; many of the principles are covered in my book Raise Your GAME Now! Delegates are taught, for example, how to use and coach applied positive psychology in their everyday lives, how to hold those awkward conversations that need to take place (such as realignment conversations with under-performing colleagues) and how to drive and measure the behaviours that are necessary to bring their company's cultural action plans alive.

There is No Risk to Rewarding the Good

Building a culture around a character ethic means that all communication and procedures need to have the intent of *looking for the good*. Employee reward and recognition systems are too often extrinsically linked – i.e. for monetary gain. When 'degrees of success' = 'amount of sales made', this becomes the system of belief that leaders use to motivate their teams. It is only carrot and stick, carrot and stick.

The vocabulary of looking for the good does not come naturally to most people. When times are hard, it can seem like a foreign language. That is why much of my methodology and training sessions, be they top down or bottom up, consist of educating delegates in applied positive psychology.

Whether they are blue collar, white collar or dog collar, male, female, young or old – people can choose to meet their basic human needs either positively or negatively. I teach techniques that empower individuals to meet their needs positively and put a personal, measurable plan in place that will allow them to sustain their growth. The same can be done in group situations, putting in place systems that allow companies to measure and sustain growth, while empowering individuals to perpetuate it through educating others.

Showing appreciation is invaluable. When was the last time you picked up the phone and told someone that they are doing a great job; when did you write a handwritten note of thanks and personally deliver it? When did you last take someone out to have a cup of coffee or buy them lunch? When did you last bring a batch of cakes into the office for no reason at all? These random acts of kindness all mean SO much to the recipients. The return on investment is off the scale and can easily be implemented throughout any company.

In my business we have a mixture of performance and contribution awards that are awarded at monthly 'Extra Mile' social gatherings; I for one have been the proud recipient of the 'Kenny's Green Shed Award' named after an ex-office junior who accidentally locked the only set of keys to our industrial storage container inside it. As a result we had to call out a metal cutting expert to break the robust lock that keeps our precious AV equipment safe. To this day we still celebrate the silly mistakes we each make every month – it's a great way of breaking the ice with newcomers – we are all only human after all!

There is a myriad of ideas for making yours a stimulating, extra mile workplace. My company installs hundreds of ideas per year, or you may want to take case-study inspiration from the Sunday Times 100 Best Companies to Work For or from organisations such as the Chartered Institute for Personal Development. What I prefer to encourage is creativity from within via suggestion schemes.

Suggestion Schemes

I was first turned onto the benefits of suggestion scheme some years ago after hearing about a team building project run by British Telecom. One of their senior executives shared with me empirical evidence that BT saved £30 million in 1999/00, £85million in 2000/01 and £36million in 2001/02 as a direct result of employee ideas. There were also benefits from reduced development time for projects which were touched by employee's ideas, and schemes and products which evolved as a consequence of employee's ideas.

An example was the SurfTime product. Other ideas were more unusual, such as the idea for providing tunnels for rabbits, which were undermining the boundary fences at some rural BT facilities.

Colleagues who are working at the coal face often know the solution to a challenge that teams at HQ have been pontificating over for months. We came across a shop manager within a multiple retailing group who responded via a suggestion scheme that he had formulated a new balanced commission scheme for colleagues which could be tracked every day in each shop using an EPOS terminal.

It turned out that the manager was actually an economics graduate. The scheme was soon implemented throughout the estate and has contributed directly to a higher quality of sale and higher average order value.

Suggestion schemes are a classic win-win – engaging colleagues to potentially make a difference to your business – and as such, ideas need to be encouraged, kept alive and rewarded.

Challenge the Bad

If you create a high performance culture where you are naturally looking for the good in your workforce, then realigning the more negative behaviours becomes far simpler to sort out. Realignment is an integral part of both creating a change – turning around the disengaged – and sustaining discipline.

If your line managers are regularly congratulating their colleagues for the excellent work they do, the rapport they build will mean that the colleagues will be far more likely to desire to reproduce this behaviour to gain more positive feedback. The managers will then be far more confident to have the more difficult conversations and the colleagues will be more receptive to those areas in which their behaviours require realigning.

> *'Uniting the forces' means installing behaviours, systems and processes that bring a company's mission statement and values to life.*

> *Keeping it alive, continuous monitoring of progress and measuring ROI becomes achievable at this stage through the introduction of a real time management system.*

> *Can you identify potential 'change agents' or Extra Mile ambassadors in your business, with the character to communicate an Extra Mile ethos?*

> *Do line managers congratulate colleagues for the excellent work they do?*

Chapter 5
Drilling It In

"Continuous effort – not strength or intelligence – is the key to unlocking our potential."

Winston Churchill

In many ways, building a business is analogous to running a well trained army. Once the strategy is in place and the forces united, action is required. This is what I refer to as 'drilling it in', the third stage of the Extra Mile Model. Excuse the military term, but it perfectly captures the process of memorizing certain actions through repetition until the action becomes instinctive.

Communication Network

"The single biggest problem in communication is the illusion that it has taken place."

George Bernard Shaw

Once a change is ignited, a colleague network must be put into place to drill the 'new way' in. Through the network, behavioural policy cascades through the organisation, ideally with an in-house sponsor who reports back to the top, and receives the CEO's full support and attention. Once information is flowing effectively into every corner of the business, sustainability of change becomes a reality.

The ownership of channels is crucial – as it will be the owners that set the standards and manage the reporting. 'Cultural ambassadors' at the frontline of the business should be empowered to temperature check progress in their area of focus, and arrange extra coaching if needed. These same channels can be used to monitor and measure the 'softer'

KPIs of a change (e.g. those relating to colleague data, surveys and customer surveys) which, when coupled with the 'harder' fiscal measures, will give a balanced audit of the change's ongoing progress. This is where the ownership of a real time performance management system is of enormous benefit.

A caring company should take into account the fact that reading emails and navigating the company intranet will not suit everyone. I have worked in companies where weekly financials, new policies, expected behaviours and the like, are all communicated by email with no personal contact or warmth of message. Is it any wonder that these can be mistakenly or deliberately overlooked, so that they lose their power or credibility?

There is no substitute for face-to-face communication whenever possible. A CEO is not able to address everyone in an organisation at all times, but s/he should expect every unit of every organisation to host disciplined, diarised and documented colleague meetings – just like HQ. Daily team briefings and regular 'huddles' can be used to manage mood and expectations. A meeting is the most potent forum to recognise the exceptional work of individuals and teams in order to motivate them further.

Cultural ambassadors should be strong verbal communicators, as speaking on a one-to-one basis or in groups makes people feel cared for. Verbal communication will also be the means by which they will intervene to instil the sustainability of the change via one-to-ones, coaching, feeding back on surveys and performance reviews.

Networking in Adversity

Free-flowing, well-policed communication channels add value to any company. More so in times of uncertainty. Sharing information, ideas and stories is vital to creating a unity of purpose and breaking down the turf wars that usually pervade organisations that pursue 'bad profits'.

Don't protect ideas and withhold information. If you have a sales team in one part of the business that is surpassing all its targets, it makes sense for their best practice to be shared with a lesser performing team elsewhere.

I believe that in adversity, opportunity always exists. Customer habits, wobbly suppliers, competitors' tactics – all this shifting market intelligence needs to come to light and be acted upon quicker than ever before to give you competitive advantage. Win the hearts and minds of your colleagues, empower them with a responsive communication network and they will sharpen your organisation's eyes and ears.

Customer-facing to Customer-approaching

> **"** We embarked on consciously building Virgin into a brand which stood for
> quality, value, fun and a sense of challenge. We also developed these ideas
> in the belief that our first priority should be the people who work for the
> companies, then the customers, then the shareholders. Because if the staff
> are motivated then the customers will be happy, and the shareholders will
> see the benefit through the company's success. **"**
>
> *Richard Branson*

The 'drilling it in' phase is also where the rules of engagement become
very clear to everybody involved. This is where a customer-facing business
becomes a customer-approaching and customer-delighting business.

The reason why many of my projects impact so readily on the bottom
line is that we always start with the end in mind – increased quality
sales. With a confident and empowered colleague base all having fun
and communicating with each other, it becomes common practice for
colleagues to want to engage customers.

Active Ethical Selling

Within the 'drilling it in' process, I insist that all colleagues are educated
in the art of selling to customers. The trick is to educate in such a fun and
interesting way that delegates start using the material that they learn in
their everyday lives both in and outside the workplace.

The purpose of my sales seminars is not to drown people with technical
jargon that doesn't appeal or stick. Rather it's to coach them to
understand what motivates human decision-making and communication
in the first place. Such education will not only help them to understand
what makes themselves and others tick, but also give them practical
tools to affect personal change. Therefore they will be able to apply this
knowledge to their relationships with partners, family, friends, colleagues
and customers.

Within the workplace, the outcome of my sales training is to set minimum
standards to perform – standards that become acceptable, everyday
company procedures and policies.

How would it make you feel if you could walk into any of your offices or outlets, go up to any customer-facing colleague at any time, and know that they would be able to answer the following questions:

What is our company mission statement?

Give 3 examples of the types of behaviour that we should use to bring our mission statement alive?

Give 3 examples of open questions that you could use to rapport build with a customer?

How would you identify a visual, audio or kinaesthetic customer and adapt your manner accordingly?

That's what I mean by acceptable standards.

With our Active Ethical Selling Model, my company aims to encourage businesses to incorporate their mission statement, vision and values (their unique identity and selling points in the marketplace) into all their interactions with customers – whether it's a relatively simple shop floor transaction or a 'full monty' boardroom to boardroom pitch.

If the colleague is selling the company, its brand and reputation, then this needs to be done from an ethical basis – from the customer's standpoint. Rather than being solely influenced by high commission and personal benefits, we aim to teach colleagues how to genuinely provide what the customer needs in order to do the right thing. After all, the vast majority of buyers can sense whether their interests are genuinely being looked after or if someone has ulterior motives in selling a product to them. We are in the business of turning customers into Net Promoters – people that would recommend the brand to friends and family.

Honing Sales Skills

Customer-facing organisations require colleagues skilled in influencing buying decisions. Personal experience and voracious study in this area have made me an expert on delivering those skills. At the core of my training model is the process of breaking down the biggest barrier that holds colleagues back from proactively approaching clients – FEAR. Some will call it lack of desire, low esteem, lack of confidence, fear of rejection. Knowing what fear feels like and why it manifests itself, allows you to accept it and channel it towards a peak state.

> **❝**Accept fear as normal, welcome fear and go with it, treat it as a motivator, know you are learning from every situation, use it as a tool for improvement. When you are sitting by the fire in your twilight years, you won't want to regret the things you didn't do as a result of fear.**❞**
>
> *Paul Stalker*

I am convinced that colleagues must be in a peak state of performance when they come into contact with customers, because that first impression can be a deal-maker or breaker. Once we have turned customer-facing colleagues into customer-approaching colleagues, the basic elements of influencing a buying decision kick-in.

Rapport build: *Find mutual ground. Ask open questions. Show respect. Identify and match your manner to your customer's style (visual, auditory, kinaesthetic).*

Establish the need: *Match the right product or service to the customer's current buying requirement.*

Educate: *Add value by showing you know the market. Use simple market data and be proud to offer advice while representing your brand.*

Express benefits: *Paint graphic pictures of your products or services enhancing your customer's lives.*

Handle objections: *Welcome, answer and isolate objections.*

Ask for the order: *Get the timing right. What else can you use within your authority to close now?*

After sales care: *The ultimate test of whether your company is pursuing good profits or not.*

After Care in Action

I was once sitting with the managing director of a kitchen company that sold 600+ kitchens per year yet hadn't leveraged a single one of those sales by following her customers up. Not one! Heresy! Her jaw nearly hit the floor when I explained to her that the cost of acquiring a new customer is up to 6 times higher than it is to sell additionally to a current customer.

We recommended a set of follow-up procedures that became mandatory in her business. These consisted of; testimonial gathering, 'before and after' photos that were used as promotional posters and press releases, coffee mornings held at satisfied client's houses where new prospects could experience the kitchens in-situ, kitchen anniversary cards, cheese and wine evenings in the showroom to which advocates were invited to mix with new prospective purchasers, mailings with loyalty offers and so on.

Following up on customers is part and parcel of sustaining the relationship, of creating an advocate network that will in turn sustain profits. We work closely with clients to tailor a suite of follow-up tools and bonding initiatives to suit the culture of each company.

Whether you have 3 customers or 3 million, retention and recommendation fuels sustainability without wasting energy.

> *'Drilling it in' is where the Extra Mile Model is taught, absorbed and lived by the entire organisation, thanks to a strong communications network and the leadership and motivational skills of your cultural ambassadors.*

> *Our training techniques transform a customer-facing organisation into a customer-approaching one.*

> *The Active Ethical Selling Model teaches sales skills that customers would approve of.*

> *Never underestimate the power of after sales care. Does your organisation maximise this opportunity?*

NOTES

Customers

Colleagues

Attitude
Survey

Real Time/
Net Promoter
Type

Internal Net
Promoter Type

KPI'S

Performance
Reviews

Attitude
Survey

Company

Line Manager

Chapter 6
Tasting Success and Measuring Victory

Employee Engagement in Action

❝ Some £40 billion was lost in Britain last year because of poor levels of engagement. The real challenge for business is how to get more people who are not just engaged but actively engaged. ❞

**David Fairhurst,
Senior VP of People, McDonald's Restaurants**

So what can you expect from your organisation once it's primed to go the Extra Mile? Our experiences with an international retailing giant demonstrate the incredible transformation that comes when change is embraced. Real success can be experienced by all the stakeholders, and that success can be measured.

Before we began working with this retailer, its huge workforce was dangerously disengaged, effectively damaging the company from within. On visiting several sites I was hardly ever approached to be helped or served. Colleagues rarely acknowledged each other. Sales opportunities were being haemorrhaged left, right and centre.

By my reckoning in this company at least one in three colleagues were actively disengaged, equating to over £100 million of wages poorly invested in the human asset.

Management style was poor, and although training was adequate it was largely operations-focused and there was no method of measuring and tracking effectiveness. Trainers' accountability stopped as soon as they moved onto the next store in their region. People performance – the ability to lead and motivate a workforce through understanding the human condition – was being overlooked.

A turning point in the first store we worked with was achieving attitudinal change in disengaged, cynical staff members. During a 'uniting the forces' session, one man – we call him Turnaround Ted – publicly shook off his negativity and began to embrace the culture of communication, mutual support and going the extra mile. Based on what we learnt in Ted's store, we developed a system of behaviours that would ensure a focus on better communication between colleagues, friendly customer contact, and operational procedures being conducted with minimum fuss.

The improvement in people performance across several stores was tracked and measured by a balanced scorecard of KPIs, which took engagement, customer feedback, operations and sales into account.

Everybody knew exactly what best practice looked like; they knew the exact words to use when greeting a customer and how to take them to a product. They knew exactly what questions to ask of the customer and they knew how to give real-time feedback to their colleagues. If they saw someone doing well, they would verbally congratulate them, and mechanisms were put in place to publicly reward and recognise. Inappropriate behaviour was realigned through coaching and mentoring.

As the 'softer' metrics such as the colleague and customer satisfaction scores grew exponentially, so did the harder measures. For example, from not reaching target in 30 weeks one store surpassed target for 21 out of the next 22 weeks.

Vital Statistics

Back in 1994 James Heskett and his team at the Harvard Business School created the holy grail of Service-Profit Chain models:

Employee satisfaction → employee retention → employee productivity → service value → customer satisfaction → customer loyalty → profitability and growth.

Or as I prefer to simplify it:

Extra mile colleagues → extra mile customers → good profits.

Heskett didn't elaborate on how to put his theory into practice and measure it. But after many years, models have been developed to allow business leaders to measure enough data throughout every step of the service-profit chain to attach a potential Return On Investment to it. 'Measuring victory' is the final quadrant of my Extra Mile Model.

Discounts, promotions, advertising campaigns, sales team competitions and monetary bonuses are all tactical, corporate steroids that can be rolled out quickly. The ROI is easy to measure. Employee engagement – your colleagues going the extra mile – takes a little more effort to measure.

Measuring every step of the way consists of:

Measuring Colleagues

This can be achieved through regular attitude surveys, internal colleague to colleague surveys, performance reviews and traditional output measures such as sales against target (as depicted in our measuring model on p.44). The purpose of such measurement is firstly to understand trends so that they can be proactively managed and secondly, to measure the effectiveness of the line managers in doing so.

A large barrier to understanding the effectiveness of colleagues and managers is the unwillingness of people to offer necessary, constructive criticism. Honest feedback pinpoints trends both good and bad. It's the job of your cultural ambassadors/line managers to act on feedback, to praise the good and challenge the bad. In this way they will be able to influence attrition, absenteeism, disciplinary and shrinkage outputs. ROI.

Measuring Training

All training and educational pieces – whether it's a technical course, a health and safety course, confidence or induction training – need to be measured. How? All your training should have an outcome, purpose and action and these criteria should be scored and fed back by the participants.

If you introduce a new range of products and hold workshops to educate your teams how to sell their features and benefits to your customers, you should measure how successful that training has been against other control groups. Your trainers should be accountable. ROI.

Measuring Customer Experience

Regular real time customer insight measured through NPS (or similar), supplemented by more detailed or tactical exit surveys and client follow-ups, is the way forward. Try to engage the customer in contributing to your brand reputation at all times.

Track your promoters and your detractors to produce a clear measure of your organisation's performance in your customers' eyes. In his book, 'The Ultimate Question' Fred Reichheld's analysis shows that, on average, increasing a Net Promoter Score by a dozen points versus competitors can double a company's growth rate. A company can now hold colleagues accountable for treating customers right and measure their ongoing progress. ROI.

All these measurements have a growth value and that's before we have even considered tracking the hard financial measures.

Then Measure the Financial Wins

In my view harder measures are the by-product of the Extra Mile Model but, of course, validate the change process, and give projections of the kind of sustainable business you can begin to build. And in no uncertain terms, they will confirm your organisation's long-term future.

A few months from initial implementation of the Extra Mile Model, clients can expect to see significant KPI improvements: Sales targets consistently being hit, sales increases versus budget flying, average transaction values up, attrition, absenteeism and shrinkage down.

Extra mile colleagues drive extra mile customers drive good profits.

> *We believe in installing structured, tried and tested systems to measure colleague attitudes and performance, brand alignment, training effectiveness and the customer experience, alongside all the financial KPIs you'd expect.*
>
> *All this can be sustained through a real time performance management system.*
>
> *Are you accurately measuring both 'soft' and 'hard' elements of your business in order to constantly improve performance?*
>
> *Are you ready to make your colleagues accountable for treating customers right?*

Digging
for
Victory

Measuring
Victory

Uniting
the
Forces

Drilling
it in

Chapter 7
Closing The Loop

I passionately believe that engaged colleagues drive and deliver performance. From the outset of every project that I work on, my goal is to present irrefutable proof to my clients that increased engagement in their companies will equal increased business performance, delivering robust ROI.

To define what success looks like for each client, to measure and track it is non-negotiable. Key measures of success may be turnover, revenue, sales growth, customer service and loyalty, staff retention, absenteeism, shrinkage and so on. Clear measurement means that I can repay the faith in those companies that hire me by often aligning my fees to results.

Sustainable growth is guaranteed if the Extra Mile Model is properly researched, embraced, drilled in and managed and measured over time. Over the last 7 years, my company has compiled an engagement database of thousands of employees across 35+ organizations in the UK. The headline findings make fascinating reading:

> *The share price of organisations with highly engaged colleagues rose by an average of 16% compared with an industry average of 6%.*

> *In companies where engagement levels are 75%+, average total shareholders' return was up to 3 times higher than those with engagement levels of circa 50%. Those companies with engagement levels below 30% posted negative shareholder returns.*

> *Business units with high engagement had average absenteeism rates of less than 4% whilst those units with low engagement experienced average absenteeism rates in excess of 8.5%.*

> *Manufacturing companies with high engagement experience staff turnover of circa 4%. Those with low engagement experience staff turnover of circa 15%.*

Within the database is a discount hardware chain. Its top quartile of stores with the highest employee retention rates enjoyed 120% more sales and 58% higher profits than the bottom quartile. Happy, empowered staff want to stay in their jobs, and they will perform at their peak.

In Search of Debbie and Doug

In life most people want the opportunity to go the extra mile. Doing the right things, achieving goals, making the effort is instinctive, rewarding and life-affirming.

Extra milers are all around us and I love celebrating what they do. As my team and I put the finishing touches to this book, South-East England had just had the worst snow it has seen for 18 years, causing all London buses to be pulled from service and the closure of Heathrow's runways. Trading on the London Stock Exchange was thinner than normal, and all over the country businesses ground to a halt.

The Federation of Small Businesses estimated 20% of the UK's working population, or 6.4 million people, did not make it to work and the disruption would cost UK businesses over £1.2 billion. Ouch. But in the midst of this gloom, two beacons of light grabbed my attention:

Debbie Does Dialysis

Firstly, renal nurse Debbie Noble, 49, walked nine miles through deep snow two days in a row to help a patient, Steph Crawford, fearing she could die without treatment. Mrs Crawford, 45, from Ewell, Surrey, suffers from kidney failure. She could not drive to her usual dialysis centre in Kingston, and ambulances could not reach her as roads were blocked by snow.

Steph told the papers: "What Debbie did was amazing. She says it is just her job but not many people would have got hiking boots and waterproof trousers on and gone out in 14 inches of snow."

Debbie's explanation? "Walking home in the snow with the moon shining was one of those moments that you store up for a rainy day."

Doug Does Dunlop's

Meanwhile, in equally treacherous conditions, realising that all of the rural roads around his home were blocked, 50 year-old Doug Fisher decided to walk the 5 miles from Manuden in Essex and still arrived in time for Monday morning opening at The Outdoor Wear Shop in Bishop's Stortford.

Doug, who has served at the shop for 7 years, was delighted to report to us that business on the day was, as he had anticipated, 'very brisk'. He had helped to sell over 80 pairs of Wellington Boots and had 'done a roaring trade in fleeces'. 'As an outdoor specialist retailer,' said Doug, 'what sort of impression would we be giving our customers if we didn't turn up for work on one of the very days that our services would most be needed? End of story!'

Well that's not quite the end of the story is it? To paraphrase Sir Winston Churchill, Doug and Debbie saw 'the opportunity in every difficulty'. They are outstanding individuals and an inspiration to us all. Both are soon to be installed as founder members of the Paul Stalker 'Extra Mile Club'.

Corporate extra milers such as Julian Richer, Charles Dunstone and Richard Branson will aim to deliver long term growth, aka 'good' profits, and in so doing will recognize that their unique assets truly are their people – intrinsically motivated people that care for the customer. The secret is to lead, breed and feed people like Doug and Debbie. And keep on doing it.

I hope that this book has articulated, through my experiences, what I believe going the extra mile looks like. I call the elements of my Extra Mile Model 'digging for victory', 'uniting the forces', 'drilling it in' and 'measuring victory'. You may wish to use different terminology, but one thing's for sure; with Grandad Jacks, Debbies and Dougs by your side, the taste of success couldn't be sweeter.

❝ *Come then, let us go forward together with our united strength.* **❞**
Winston Churchill

We're here to help organisations prosper through the empowerment and engagement of their people.

Our goal is to present irrefutable proof to our clients that increased engagement in their companies will equal increased business performance from higher sales and profits to less attrition, absenteeism and shrinkage.

Every company has 'extra milers' in its midst. Who are the Debbies and Dougs in your organisation, and what can they help you achieve?